Entertaining Hawaiian Style
The How To Book of Hawaiian Luaus

Written by Patricia L. Fry
Illustrated by Ron Croci

Third Edition

ISLAND HERITAGE PUBLISHING

Dedication

*In loving memory of
Ethel Eddy
who delighted in teaching
others the ways of
her people.*

Contents

Introduction to a Luau

Chapter 1	Let's Plan a Luau		10

  Make This a Togetherness Project
  How to Choose the Perfect Party Place
  The Etiquette and How-to of Invitations

Chapter 2   The Art of Decorating for a Luau   14
  Tips for Preparing the Luau Site
  Naturally Elegant Table Decorations
  Yard, Patio and Pool-Side Decorating Ideas
  The Romance of the Lei
  Tips for Stringing Fresh Flower Leis
  How to Make Paper Leis
  Tips for Creating Island Attire

Chapter 3   Popular Island Recipes   25
  Tips for Planning Your Menu
  Tantalizing Appetizers
  Deliciously Hot Side-Dishes
  Scrumptious Salads
  Additional Accompaniments
  Additional Helps

Chapter 4   Delightful Hawaiian Punch Recipes   40
  Tips for Making Punch

Chapter 5   How to Cook a Luau Pig   43
  First Comes the Pig
  What Size Pig?
  Kalua (Roasted Underground) Pig
  Creating the Pit
  The Gravel Alternative
  How to Prepare and Roast the Pig
  Check List for Cooking in a Pit

Pig On A Spit
When is the Pork Done?
Above the Ground Pit Barbecue
Build a Pit Above the Ground
Basted Pork Barbecue
The Redwood Box Cooker Method
Oven Roasted Suckling Pig
Stuffing a Pig
Serving the Pork
Tips for Tending the Pig

Chapter 6	Entertaining Your Luau Guests	63
Chapter 7	A Hawaiian Language Lesson	66
Chapter 8	Sundry Host/Hostess Tips How to Handle Difficult Guests Tips for Staying Cool	72

Index to Recipes   76

Warning -- Disclaimer

These cooking methods and these recipes have been used successfully and satisfactorily by at least one group and in most cases many groups of party-givers and party-goers. You, too, will have a successful and safe luau experience if you use common sense and common safety measures when attempting any of these techniques and recipes.

Take care in handling food. Food items should not be kept at room or outside temperature for extended periods of time. The Tenth edition of the *Better Homes and Gardens ® New Cookbook* recommends that cooked or chilled foods left at room temperature longer than two hours should be discarded.

Always wash hands, working area, platters and utensils with soap after working with raw meat or poultry.

The editors of the *Better Homes and Gardens ® New Cookbook* suggest that if you have any questions about meat and poultry handling or safety, call the U.S. Department of Agriculture's Meat and Poultry hot line: 800/535-4555. In the Washington DC area, call 447-3333.

The cooking times and temperatures recommended in this book are actual cooking times and temperatures used successfully by us and/or others. As you would do with any recipe from any cookbook, however, we recommend that you use your common sense and good judgment in preparing your luau. Make sure the pork is done before serving it even if it has to cook longer than we recommend.

We've seen pigs that were burned to a crisp when removed from the pit after the recommended time (caused by improperly wrapped pork and too much heat inside) and we've seen them come out too rare (not enough heat inside), but mostly we've served mouth-watering, fall-off-the-bone pork that had everyone coming back for more.

Where there's fire there's heat ... and heat can burn. **Use extreme care in building and working with all methods of cooking that we recommend. Never leave an open pit unattended. Never leave an open fire unattended. Never leave a hot barbecue or any other outdoor cooking apparatus unattended.**

Introduction to A Luau

The luau is a Hawaiian feast typically prepared to honor holidays and to celebrate weddings, birthdays, house warmings and just about any other occasion. Just as mainland Americans traditionally socialize around a Western barbecue theme and our neighbors south-of-the-border customarily celebrate with a fiesta, for Islanders, it's the luau. Like the barbecue and the fiesta, the luau is generally held outdoors. Food and drink are served at all three of these gatherings. And everyone usually has a good time. This, however, is where the similarities end.

Mainlanders typically serve their guests steak or hamburgers, chili beans, potato salad, corn on the cob, French bread, homemade ice cream, soda pop and beer. Mexicans offer their traditional delights: tamales, refried beans, tortillas, and margaritas. And Islanders feast on roast pork, sweet potatoes, fish, rice, fresh fruits and light, fruity punches.

To decorate for a barbecue, one might toss checkered table- cloths over wooden picnic tables, set them with decorator paper plates and scatter a few bales of hay around for seating. In Mexico, they set the tables with colorful Mexican pottery and further adorn the party area with hundreds of large, handmade paper flowers. Hawaiians use an abundance of fresh fruit, fresh flowers and large crisp leaves or fern fronds in their luau decorations.

Guests attending a barbecue wear their comfortable, casual Sunday afternoon clothes -- jeans or shorts and tee shirts. Typical attire for a Mexican fiesta is brightly colored cotton dresses for the women and loose-fitting cotton shirts for the men. Luau-goers wear colorful Hawaiian-print dresses and shirts. The men might also don a straw hat while the women tuck a fresh flower behind an ear (the left ear if she's "taken" and the right ear if she's available.)

At a backyard barbecue, guests often play horseshoes, Frisbee or volleyball. After the meal, they might have an old-fashioned sing-a-long. Typical fiesta entertainment includes lively dance exhibitions and a pinata. In Hawaii, luau guests often participate in rhythmic music-making and swaying Island dances.

Does this description of a luau make you yearn to visit Hawaii? There's no need to go to that extreme to participate in one of these Island events. You can have your own luau – even on the mainland – even at home.

Within the pages of this book you'll find everything you need to know about planning and presenting a luau including instructions for several different methods of cooking a whole pig. You'll learn how to prepare a variety of Hawaiian side-dishes, how to create spectacular decorations from easy-to-find materials and the secret of making beautiful fresh flower leis. I'll offer tips for accommodating a large number of guests and even help you select your luau attire for little or no cost.

So put a Don Ho CD in your player, curl up with this book and start planning what could be the event of the season – *your mainland luau*.

1. Let's Plan A Luau

In the beginning there was an idea. Then there had to be motivation. What motivates you to want to have a luau? It could be that your club or organization needs a fund-raising event. Perhaps you'd like to use the Hawaiian theme for a wedding reception or birthday party. Maybe you're simply in the mood to entertain a few or a bunch of friends and you want to do it Hawaiian style.

A luau can be hosted by as few or as many people as you want to involve. If the guest list is comprised of 25 people or less, you could easily go it alone. If you want to entertain 50 people, ask a friend or two to help. When the guest list mounts upwards toward 100 or more people, you may want to have several heads, hands and kitchens at your disposal.

We used to hold an annual luau at our home for between 80 and 125 guests and we would ask three or four other couples to share in the planning, the work and the expense. Of course, each couple was invited to add their friends' names to the guest list, as well.

Make This a Togetherness Project

We found that working with friends to get ready for the event was almost as much fun as the luau itself. And having the support of others gave us more resources to draw from and more confidence to attempt things we might not try on our own: learning and performing the hula to entertain our guests, for example, and stringing our own fresh flower leis.

If you decide to plan your luau as a group, ask each person to keep a record of their party-related expenses. Save receipts for decoration supplies, recipe ingredients, paper goods, plastic leis or anything else you might purchase for the luau. When the luau is over, add up the expenses, deduct the cost of any items a participant wishes to keep (tiki torches or Hawaiian recordings, for example). Divide the total by the number of participants and charge or reimburse the couples accordingly.

There's plenty of planning involved in putting on a large luau. And sometimes the larger the group of party-planners, the more complicated the decision-making process. If you find that when discussing ideas for the luau you're going around issues and not resolving anything because of too much input, whittle out smaller committees to decide specific details.

Some of you can review recipes and plan the menu, while others organize and arrange for decorations and still others might be in charge of locating and selecting a pig, for example.

Many typical luau dishes require a great deal of time to prepare. Here are three suggestions for using your time and combined energies most effectively in the food preparation process:

1. Work together in assembly-line fashion to do the necessary paring, chopping, mixing and cooking.

2. Assign each couple one or two recipes to prepare in their own homes.

3. Ask guests to contribute something – a fruit bowl, rice dish or coconut or pineapple dessert, for example.

Preparing the luau site is another time-consuming process with which you could use some help, particularly if the event is to be held at your home. Most likely you'll want to do some special yard clean-up projects and rearrange things to better accommodate your guests. This won't seem so overwhelming if you have a committee working with you. Their participation will be appreciated during the after-luau clean-up, too.

How to Choose the Perfect Party Place

Whether you decide to include others in the planning stages of your luau or go it on your own, the first step is deciding where to hold it. It could be in someone's backyard, at a community park or even in a rented hall. The at-home backyard patio or pool-side luau is ideal because a tropical theme can be more easily used and there are fewer outside distractions than there are at a public park, for example. Also, there is easy access to refrigeration and other conveniences.

When you hold a luau away from home, it's seldom possible to cook a pig under the ground unless you cook it ahead of time and transport it to the luau site. This book does include instructions for cooking a pig in a barbecue pit, however, which can be done just about anywhere.

The Etiquette and How-to of Invitations

Although the phone call may be a suitable method of inviting guests to an intimate luau, a large luau requires invitations. You can save money and begin setting the mood for the luau by gathering your committee together to design, make and address the invitations.

Of course, we were doing luaus pre-computer age and we created our invitations by drawing Hawaiian theme designs on colored paper.

Today, however, I would design the invitations in my computer using clip art or photographs and have them copied at a local print shop.

To further entice guests to attend your luau, include your menu on the invitation. For example: "We will be serving authentic pit-barbecued Kalua Pig, Fran's Tempting Chicken Hawaiian, Crab-Rice Salad Ala Allan, tons of fresh fruit, To-Die-For Coconut Ice Cream and Evelyn's Watch-Out Volcano Punch."

The etiquette of responding to an R.S.V.P. seems to be passé. As a rule of thumb, if your guest list is 50 or more, you can expect a little over half to attend. The percentage of attendees for a more intimate affair is closer to 98%.

2. The Art of Decorating For A Luau

It's practically impossible not to feel the lure of the Islands at a well-arranged Hawaiian luau. The brilliant costumes and colorful decorations awaken the spirit even upon one's arrival. The use of fresh flowers throughout the party site appeals to one's sense of romance. And the sweet songs of Hawaii playing softly in the background can't help but touch the guests' heartstrings.

It's not difficult and it's actually rather fun to create an atmosphere for a luau. And the place to start is with the basic design of the party area.

Tips for Preparing the Luau Site

Providing pool-side or patio seating for each guest at a gathering of 40 or more, may not be necessary. While some people will plant themselves and stay planted throughout the affair, most others drift and mingle. Furnish as much seating as you have room for by borrowing or renting folding and/or stackable chairs. But for a larger group, don't feel that you have to have a chair for each guest.

Table-seating is another matter. You'll want to arrange seating so that everyone dines together, particularly if there will be entertainment during or after dinner. If your luau is confined to one area -- a large patio, a tennis court, an expanse of lawn or a freshly mowed field, for example -- you'll set up your tables there. Where you have enough room, you may choose to serve punch and cocktails in one area and the meal in another.

For a more uniform appearance, rent matching square or round tables or large buffet tables and chairs. If you want to save money, borrow an array of picnic tables, card tables and utility tables from neighbors and friends. If you prefer an air of authenticity, create tables by placing sheets of plywood on large concrete bricks (8" x 8" x 16") stacked two high at the corners and lay rattan beach mats on the ground around the tables for seating. Cover the plywood tables with rattan mats, plain white butcher paper, colored crepe paper, rented table cloths or lengths of colorful fabric cut to fit the tables.

Naturally Elegant Table Decorations
---

1. Lay sprays of greenery down the middle of the table and either scatter fresh rose petals over the greens or, at the last minute, tuck fresh flowers amongst them.
    ### Suggested Greens
    Ivy
    Fern
    Palm fronds
    Banana, philodendron or canna leaves
    Mimosa, pepper or magnolia tree sprays

NOTE: Look around your yard, your neighborhood and friends' yards a week or so before the luau to see what type of greens will be available. Cuttings from most any slow-wilting vine, large-leaf plant or attractive tree should work.

2. Create center pieces using tropical fruit. Arrange whole fruit amidst selected greens which are placed down the center of the table, or stack whole fruits in mounds with greens and flowers tucked around them. You can display whole fruit in monkey pod bowls or cut fruit in bite-size pieces and serve in watermelon or pineapple boats.

Suggested Fruit to Use in Decorating

Bananas	Papayas
Mangoes	Pineapples
Grapes	Melons
Oranges	Apples
Peaches	Apricots
Kiwi	Pears

3. Arrange bouquets of fresh flowers on each table. If you want an air of authenticity, order anthuriums, the large, red, plastic-like flower of Hawaii, through your local florist. Anthuriums run about $4.00 to $6.00 each on the mainland, but they do make spectacular centerpieces.

4. Float candles in bowls of colored water and use them among the fruit or flower centerpieces.

5. Lay a fresh flower at each table setting. Use magnolias, orchids, daisies, hibiscus or lilies, for example.

6. You can also use seashells, Hawaiian shell and pod necklaces, straw hats, large paper flowers, lengths of Hawaiian print fabric, netting (such as a fisherman's net), small ukuleles or paper leis in the centerpiece arrangement.

7. Create elegant centerpieces by filling vases with large sprays of fresh greenery, decorate them with shell necklaces and place them in mounds of sand strewn with seashells, glitter and colorful paper leis.

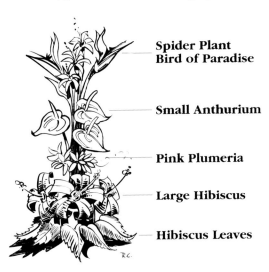

Spider Plant
Bird of Paradise

Small Anthurium

Pink Plumeria

Large Hibiscus

Hibiscus Leaves

Yard, Patio and Pool-Side Decorating Ideas

The key to decorating for a luau is color. You'll also want to think tropical. The following ideas will help you get started.

1. Decorate outside house walls or fences with arrangements of large leaves and fern fronds, Hawaiian travel posters (obtained through local travel agents or airlines) or coarse netting and shells.

2. Create over-sized bouquets of cannas, day lilies, iris, crepe myrtle, bird of paradise, bougainvillea, acacia sprays or branches of fruit tree blossoms.

3. Place potted ferns, palms or orchids around. (You may be able to borrow or rent these.)

4. Decorate porch or patio cover columns by spiraling flower ropes around the length of them. Make flower ropes by wrapping sprays of fresh, dried or silk flowers together along a length of cord with florist's tape. Reinforce limp stems with florist's wire. Use baby's-breath, hibiscus, carnations, daisies, camellias, asters, dahlias, lilies, zinnias or marigolds.

5. Place tiki torches around the grounds and along the driveway.

6. Float candles or fresh flowers in the pool or a child's wading pond.

7. Display photos of past luaus on a free-standing easel. For added interest, trim photos, mount them on colored paper which is cut into Hawaiian theme shapes (pineapples, ukuleles, hula girls, etc.) and add captions.

8. Build a grass shack on the luau site. Cover a simple wood frame with wire mesh and tuck banana, canna or palm leaves or leafy bamboo stalks, for example, into the wire. This would be a great way to camouflage a portable potty.

9. Ask friends and neighbors to rummage through their closets, attics, garages or back lots for island-related items that could be incorporated into your decorations. For example, Polynesian masks, a crude wooden raft, part of an old boat, a set of oars, a mounted fish, a grass skirt, canes of bamboo, a surf board or a pair of feather gourds.

The Romance of the Lei

The lei is a floral necklace worn by both men and women in Hawaii for most any occasion. Wear a lei loosely around the neck so that it drapes down in the front and the back.

If the guest list isn't too large, make fresh-flower leis the evening before the event and store them in plastic bags in the refrigerator over night. Present one to each guest as they arrive for the luau. Or give each guest a box of blossoms (or ask them to bring their own flowers) and provide lei-making lessons as part of the event.

Choose flowers that can go without water for 4 or 5 hours. Suitable mainland flowers that can be used for leis or crowns (head garlands) include orchids, stock, carnations, chrysanthemums, daisies, roses, asters, Martha Washington geraniums, ice plant flowers, dahlias, marigolds or most any other hardy flower. I particularly like the full lei one gets when using marigolds, however, their strong scent offends some wearers. You can also create attractive leis by stringing magnolia leaves.

If you have a large guest list, you might want to make paper leis a few weeks ahead of time -- and then make fresh flower host/hostess leis the morning of the luau. Islanders recommend picking flowers for your lei early in the morning before the sun wipes the dew from the blossoms.

If you must purchase flowers, seek out roadside stands as they typically offer fresh flowers at reduced prices.

Tips for Stringing Fresh Flower Leis

Cut the stems from the flowers. For carnations, cut off part of the green, leaving just enough to hold the flower together. Using a 45-inch length of crochet thread and a 2-inch needle, string full flowers, such as carnations, most chrysanthemums, roses and marigolds, through the center of the head to the base. Push the blossoms close together for full leis or crowns.

String daisies, ice plant flowers and other flat blossoms sideways. For a lei, use 30 to 60 blossoms, depending on their size. For a crown, use 15 to 25 flowers.

How to Make Paper Leis

Cut folded crepe paper into several 2-inch or 3-inch strips. Unfold the crepe paper strips and draw the needle through each one using a long gathering stitch. Push the crepe paper down on the thread into gathers as you go. When you've reached the desired length, twist the paper strips into a rounded shape and tie the ends of the string together.

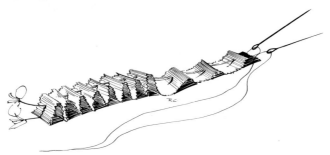

Tips for Creating Island Attire

Your guests dressed in brilliant Hawaiian attire will add the finishing touches to your luau decorations. You'll also want to dress in an Island theme, and there's no need to spend a lot of money on new clothes for the occasion.

Consider these options:

- Borrow something to wear. Anyone who has ever been to Hawaii has some item of appropriate Island wear hanging in the back of their closet.

- Rent a grass skirt from a costume rental outlet.

- Browse through local thrift stores to find a good deal on someone else's Hawaiian theme cast-aways.

- Create a Hawaiian look from your own closet.

For a woman:

- Wear a colorful flowing skirt, plain peasant blouse and sandals.

- Dress up a plain skirt and blouse or solid-colored dress with a bright sash tied around the waist and hanging nearly the length of the skirt.

- Buy Hawaiian print fabric and make a loose-fitting muu muu, a sarong or a skirt.

- Creatively wrap a piece of floral print fabric around your hips or tie it at one shoulder over a bathing suit or a pair of spandex bicycle shorts and top.

23

A man can wear either the traditional Hawaiian shirt with trousers, shorts or a grass skirt, or he can wear cut-off jeans or colorful bathing trunks and a tank top.

Accessorize with an outrageous straw hat, shell necklaces, fresh flower leis, head garlands and/or anklets.

3. Popular Island Recipes

The centerpiece of any luau is the roasted pig. Guests typically gather around the fire pit eagerly awaiting the unearthing of the pig, anxious for their first taste of succulent pork. But the pig does not stand alone. To complete a luau feast, the appropriate accompaniments must be added.

What is considered true "Hawaiian cuisine" is not actually rooted in any one pure island culture, but reflects the culinary traditions of many of the cultures that discovered the Pacific Islands over the centuries.

Polynesians, thought to have been the first to settle Hawaii around 200 - 500 AD, brought pigs, chickens, bananas, coconuts, bamboo, gourds, sweet potatoes, sugar cane and taro.

When the Chinese came to work on the sugar plantations, they introduced many new vegetables to Islanders and taught them to cut vegetables and meat into small pieces before cooking them.

Japanese plantation workers contributed enormously to the Hawaiian Island culture through their art and simplistic style as well as their eating habits. They, reportedly, introduced new foods and new cooking methods, including the original barbecue.

The Portuguese came to the Islands around 1879 bringing their traditional spices. And travelers from India are responsible for the addition of curry in some of the old Island dishes.

Around the turn of the century, Koreans and Filipinos arrived, bringing with them their seasoning traditions. And, of course, early Spanish and New England settlers left their culinary mark.

Tips for Planning Your Menu

For a recent luau, we served 100 guests for under $500. Before shopping for ingredients, we compared prices between a major grocery chain market and a wholesale outlet where we could buy in bulk. We found that, while the wholesale outlet was cheaper on some items, there was little or no price difference with most ingredients.

Our menu consisted of appetizers: Salmon Stuffed Tomatoes, Pineapple-Shrimp Pupus, a vegetable platter, Crab-Rice Salad, a fresh fruit bowl, green salad with honey dressing, Long Rice, Chicken Hawaiian, Pit-Roasted Pork, yams and rolls. We figured 2 cup serving of each side dish, 1 piece of chicken and about 1 pound of pork (dressed weight) per person, which left everyone satisfied, with no leftovers.

Use the following recipes and your imagination to add elegant but simple side dishes to your luau feast.

𝒯antalizing 𝒜ppetizers

Begin your luau feast with pupus – Hawaiian hors d'oeuvres. Platters of pupus (*poo poos*) can be served while guests await the unveiling of the roasted pig.

ℰasy 𝒥sland 𝓜eatballs

Serves 50

- 6 pounds leanest ground beef
- 2 cups soy sauce
- 1 cup water
- 3/4 cup brown sugar
- 1 clove garlic, minced
- 2 1/2 teaspoons powdered ginger
- Food picks

Form meat into 1-inch balls. Place in a single layer on shallow baking pans. Combine remaining ingredients and pour about half of the sauce over the meatballs.

(Add more sauce while cooking if necessary). Cook for 1 hour uncovered at 275°.

This recipe can be prepared up to two days prior to the luau, providing the meat used is very fresh to start with. To store, cool cooked meatballs, place them in a large casserole dish, pour remaining sauce over them, cover and refrigerate. To serve, heat meatballs and sauce in oven or microwave and serve with food picks.

Salmon Stuffed Tomatoes

———

60 servings

    60 cherry tomatoes
    1 $1/2$ cans salmon (14 $3/4$ ounce can)
    2 green onions, thinly sliced
    1 teaspoon celery salt

With a sharp knife, slice tops off tomatoes and just enough of the bottom so that the tomato doesn't tip. Scoop out the tomato pulp and mash. Mix together pulp, flaked salmon, onion and celery salt. Chill mixture and tomato shells. Just before serving, stuff salmon mixture into tomato shells.

Pineapple-Shrimp Pupus

———

Approximately 100 servings

    4 large cans pineapple chunks (reserve liquid)
    2 - 12 ounce packages shrimp, cooked
    $1/2$ cup brown sugar
    2 tablespoons soy sauce
    $1/4$ cup chili sauce (such as Heinz)
    Food picks

Place one pineapple chunk and one cooked shrimp on each food pick. Cover and chill until serving time. For a dipping sauce, combine the reserved pineapple juice with remaining ingredients. Mix well and serve.

Sweet and Sour Pork

50 - 60 servings

3 pounds pork steak cut into 1-inch cubes
1 cup corn starch
$1/2$ teaspoon salt
$1/2$ teaspoon garlic salt
2 eggs
$1/4$ cup milk
1 can pineapple chunks (reserve liquid)
1 green pepper
2 stalks celery
1 brown or white onion
$1/2$ cup vinegar
1 teaspoon sugar
2 tablespoons soy sauce
Food picks (optional)

Blend together corn starch, salt, garlic salt, eggs and milk. Dip meat pieces into this batter and deep fry in oil until done. Lay meat on absorbent paper towels to drain. If fresh, cooked meat can be stored in the refrigerator for up to 2 days. Before serving, drain the pineapple chunks, reserving the liquid. Cut green pepper, celery and onion in diagonal pieces. Place cooked meat, vegetables and pineapple in a heavy skillet. Mix together: vinegar, sugar, soy sauce and pineapple juice and add to the ingredients in the skillet. Heat, stirring constantly. When the pork is hot, it is ready to serve. Serve with food picks as an appetizer or over rice as a main dish.

There are any number of other pupu possibilities. Just think tropical and use your imagination. Arrange a fresh fruit platter, serve crisp vegetable sticks or pour sweet and sour sauce over frankfurter bites.

Delicious Hot Side-Dishes

Rice is a Hawaiian staple that should also be a part of a mainland luau. Here are a few of the favorites we served at our annual luaus thanks to our Hawaiian friend Ethel Eddy.

Fried Rice

For 25 people

5 pounds (12 cups) rice
(not the pre-cooked type)

1 cup pre-cooked (leftover) pork or beef
3 tablespoons oil
2 tablespoons soy sauce
$3/4$ teaspoon sugar
2 eggs
1 bunch green onions, chopped
$1/2$ can water chestnuts, sliced

Wash rice until water is clear. Soak rice in 1 1/4 cups water for each 1 cup of rice for 10 - 15 minutes. (About 3 3/4 quarts water for 5 pounds of rice). Cook rice over medium heat in the same water. When water begins to boil, lower heat and cover. Continue cooking until rice is done (approximately 20 minutes). Chop meat into small pieces. Heat oil in frying pan over medium-high heat and add meat, soy sauce and sugar. Stir. Add eggs and continue stirring as they cook. Lower heat and add cooked rice, stirring constantly. Add onion and water chestnuts. When completely mixed, remove from heat and serve.

Long Rice

15 servings

6 cups fresh beef or chicken broth
1 package ($3/4$ ounce) long rice
   (saifun or bean thread -- available in the Oriental section of most markets)
2 eggs
1 $1/2$ cups chicken strips
$1/2$ cup pork strips
soy sauce (to taste)
sugar (to taste)
1 medium onion, chopped
7 mushrooms, sliced
$1/2$ can water chestnuts
1 clove garlic, minced

1 bunch green onions, sliced thin

Make a broth by boiling necks and backs of chicken or beef bones. (This can be done several days ahead.) Soak long rice in water until it is slightly pliable (about 20 minutes). Cut long rice into smaller pieces. Hard boil the eggs, chop and set aside. Cook meat in hot oil. (Meat can be cooked a few days ahead of time.) Add soy sauce, sugar and chopped onions to meat and cook until meat is tender. Add broth, mushrooms, water chestnuts and garlic to the meat mixture. When broth boils, add long rice. Long rice is done when it has absorbed most of the liquid (approximately 20 minutes). Add green onions and chopped eggs. Stir well. Keep warm until serving time.

Chicken Hawaiian

Approximately 40 servings
(A native Hawaiian prepared this delicious barbecued chicken for us one balmy evening on Waikiki Beach.)

    3 quarts soy sauce
    6 large onions, sliced
    2 whole garlic cloves, chopped

3 tablespoons powdered ginger
$3/4$ cup mustard
$3/4$ cup brown sugar
Juice from $1/2$ lemon
6 chickens cut up (or 20 legs with thighs attached)

Mix the first 7 ingredients together. Marinate the chicken in this mixture for 20 minutes and then barbecue until done. Use the same amount of marinade for larger quantities of chicken. Note: This marinade is also good with fish.

Scrumptious Salads

With a little creativity, nearly any salad can be made appropriate for a luau. Here are a few ideas for dressing up your ordinary salads Hawaiian style:

Green Salad: Make it easy on yourself and buy packaged ready-to-mix salad greens. Always wash thoroughly. Add bits of crab and top with Green Goddess salad dressing.

Linaka's Honey Dressing: Mix equal parts rice vinegar, olive or flaxseed oil and honey. Our green salad is always a big hit when we use this dressing.

Pasta Salad: Mix in tiny shrimp or other seafood and toss with a sour cream dressing.

Fruit Salad: Serve your favorite fruit salad in melon or pineapple shells.

Or adapt one of these delicious recipes for use at your luau.

Easy Hawaiian Fruit Salad

Cut any combination of these fruits into bite-size pieces:

Peaches	Pears	Kiwi
Oranges	Melons	Papaya
Pineapple	Nectarines	Mango
Bananas	Apples	Guava

Add cherries and fresh flaked coconut. Mix, chill and serve.

Luau Fruit Salad for 50

2 fresh pineapples
5 pounds apples
50 large marshmallows
6 oranges
6 pears
6 peaches
2 cups seedless grapes
2 cups walnuts
10 bananas
2 cups coconut

Cut all fruit into bite-size pieces. Combine all ingredients except walnuts, bananas and coconut. Chill. Mix in remaining ingredients just before serving. A whipping cream or yogurt dressing may be added, but is not necessary.

Make it Easy On Yourself Fruit Salad for a Crowd

Approximately 100 half-cup servings

3 one-gallon cans of Hawaiian fruit with mango and papaya (available through wholesale grocery outlets)
1 watermelon, cut into bite-size pieces or balls
1 large bunch of seedless grapes
6 kiwi

Mix together the first 3 ingredients. Slice kiwi and place decoratively on top of the fruit. Chill until serving time.

Crab-Rice Salad

Serves 25

4 cups cooked rice, cooled
4 cans crab meat, flaked
2 cans water chestnuts, sliced
1 cup slivered almonds
1 bunch green onions, thinly sliced
1 $1/2$ cups mayonnaise
$1/4$ cup vinegar
1 teaspoon oregano
1 teaspoon salt

Combine first 5 ingredients and mix well. Combine remaining ingredients and fold into rice mixture. Chill.

Additional Accompaniments

As a rule of thumb, the more guests, the more variety you'll want in the menu. For a large group, to go along with your pupu platters, salads, fresh fruit and rice side-dishes, you may also want to add roasted yams.

Yams

Whole yams are a familiar addition to a Hawaiian feast. They can be baked in the oven or roasted in the pit or in the barbecue along with the pig. Wash yams, wrap individually in foil and place in the pit with the pig or among the coals in a barbecue pit. To serve yams, cut into thirds or fourths – plan to use one yam per every three guests (10 yams for 30 people).

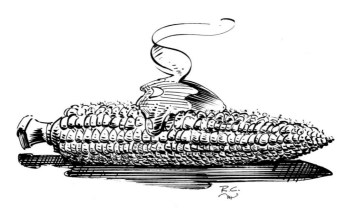

Corn on the Cob

Another popular contribution to the mainland luau is corn on the cob. Remove husks and silk. Pour about eight cans of evaporated milk, several quarts of water and a cup of sugar into a large, clean tub. Place the tub over hot coals and bring its contents to a boil. Drop the ears of corn into the tub and boil for 5 minutes.

Ethel's Laulaus

———

Fresh, washed spinach or young grape leaves
Thin strips of white fish
Thin slices of raw pork

Lay each leaf on a small square of aluminum foil. Add a strip of fish and a slice of pork to each. Gather up the edges of the foil and tightly twist. Steam until pork is cooked. For an added flair, steam them over an open fire. Place a rack in a large tub of water. Lay the laulaus on the rack above the water. Cover the tub and place over hot coals for about 2 hours. When the pork is done, the laulaus are ready to serve.

Bread

———

Fruit breads are also an excellent luau accompaniment. Make applesauce, pumpkin, pineapple, persimmon or banana breads weeks ahead of the luau and freeze. On the morning of the luau, remove the breads from the freezer. At serving time, arrange sliced bread attractively on large platters. For 50 people, you'll need 5 or 6 loaves of bread.

Additional Helps

Most people aren't prepared to serve 50 to 100 people from their kitchen. Among the items they lack are huge cooking kettles and over-sized serving bowls and trays. Use ice chests to mix large quantities of marinade and to keep meat, corn and yams warm until serving time. Rent commercial stainless steel chafing dishes (size 16" x 24") to keep salads chilled. Keep hot dishes warm in electric roasting pans. Borrow large serving bowls and trays, purchase them at thrift stores or improvise:

- Cover old cookie sheets and trays with foil.

- To serve breads, cover trays with paper doilies or cloth.

- Make a plain bowl more attractive by lining it with romaine or other leafy lettuce leaves before filling it with your chilled rice dish or salad.

- Utilize odd containers such as large decorated popcorn tins, canning kettles, turkey roasters and unused dishpans.

- For smaller portions, use melon or pineapple shells, or large washed leaves as serving bowls.

To add a touch of class to your buffet table, surround bowls and trays with rich, green leaves among which bright fresh flowers have been tucked. Suggested flowers are: hibiscus, marigolds, zinnias, asters, geraniums, gladiolus, holly hocks, cannas, sweet peas or roses. Use baby's-breath for added effect.

Decorate pale vegetable, meat or seafood pupu platters with dark green and red leafy lettuce leaves, bright red cherry tomatoes and carrot curls.

Top creamy fruit salads or molded gelatin salads with grape or cherry halves arranged in the shape of a pineapple, palm tree or other Hawaiian symbol.

Spruce up a creamy pasta salad with sprigs of fresh parsley arranged around a small centerpiece of cherry tomatoes and a sprinkling of paprika.

4. Delightful Hawaiian Punch Recipes

A standard punch bowl holds 8 quarts.

Fruity Island Punch

Approximately 60 Servings

2 quarts cranberry apple juice
1 quart orange juice
1 quart pineapple juice
3 quarts ginger ale
1 quart vodka or rum (optional)

Kahlua Punch

50 - 60 Servings

$1/2$ gallon fruit punch concentrate
   (prepared according to label directions)
2 large cans pineapple juice

1 quart ginger ale
1/2 gallon vodka
2 quarts coffee-flavored liqueur

For either punch, mix chilled juices together in large punch bowl or crock with a spigot. Add liquor and ice. Add carbonated drinks just before serving.

For a smaller group, you may want to serve exotic drinks. Following are a few suggestions.

Pineapple Daiquiri

12 Servings

2 1/4 cups pineapple juice
1/3 cup sugar
1/2 cup lime juice
2 1/4 cups rum
cracked ice

Blend all ingredients except ice in blender for 30 seconds. Gradually add ice and blend until mixture is slushy. Note: You may want to add bananas or strawberries.

Chi Chi

10 Servings

3 cups pineapple juice
2/3 cup powdered coconut
1 1/2 cups vodka
Cracked ice

Prepare same as for the daiquiri.

You may want to get together with your co-hosts/hostesses and create your own punch -- this is how the Kahlua punch recipe was created.

Tips for Making Punch

- Add carbonated beverages at serving time.

- Make pretty ice cubes or an ice ring using orange slices, pineapple chunks, cherries, edible flowers or greens or a little food coloring in your ice tray or ring.

- Have on hand at least twice as many punch cups or glasses as you think you'll need.

- Pour the first glass of punch for every guest and invite them to help themselves when they desire a refill. If you're serving alcoholic beverages, you may prefer having a responsible adult dispensing them. Consider preparing just enough of the alcoholic drinks or punch for one or two rounds and then switch to fruity ice tea, lemonade and coffee.

- When serving fancy Polynesian blender drinks to 15 or fewer guests, you can easily offer 3 or more varieties. When serving between 20-30 guests, stick with 1 or 2 choices. For 40 or more guests, you're wise to stick to a punch that can be made ahead of time.

5. How To Cook A Luau Pig

And now for the guest of honor -- the roast pig. No matter how you go about it, the pig will be the most expensive, the most time-consuming, the most worrisome and the most popular part of the luau.

Note: Not everyone who wants to cook a whole pig is interested in making their event a Hawaiian affair. Whole hog barbecuing has been a popular form of entertainment in the south U. S. for some time and that popularity is growing throughout the states. The following instructions and tips for preparing a luau pig can also be applied to whole hog barbecuing.

First Comes The Pig

Unless you happen to raise pigs or know someone who does, you probably don't have the slightest idea about how to locate a pig for your luau.

Start by checking the classified section of your newspaper and the Yellow Pages under "Livestock." Ask your local feed store owner to recommend a pig rancher in your area. Inquire at a meat market or slaughter house, Or order a U.S.D.A. federally inspected whole pig by mail.

W & G Marketing Co. Inc. in Ames, Iowa, for example, ships Iowa corn-fed sucklings and roasting pigs weighing anywhere from 10 to 150 pounds to any destination in and outside the United States.

Marvin J. Walter, president of W & G Marketing, recommends cooking a pig with the skin on for maximum quality and appearance. According to Walter, "The skin forces the internal fat to migrate through the meat as the pig cooks and this ensures a more moist and tasty product. Skinned pigs do not cook up as fast and can create a definite flaming problem when cooked in a barbecue pit."

Keep in mind that the process of de-hairing, which is necessary for a skin-on pig, is time-consuming and few slaughterhouses offer this service. If you can't find someone locally to prepare a pig with the skin on, contact a professional supplier such as W & G Marketing.

What Size Pig?

Often, even more difficult than locating a pig outlet is deciding what size pig to buy. Walter advises figuring about 1 pound per person dressed weight. According to Walter, a pig will lose 30-35% of weight in the dressing process. A 100-pound pig would dress to approximately 65-70 pounds and serve 65-70 people.

Kalua (Roasted Underground) Pig
Creating the Pit

Hawaiians roast their pork in under-ground pits using hot rocks to generate the heat. Lava rock, which is abundant on the Islands, is well suited to the extreme heat within the imu or cooking pit. If you can't find or purchase lava rock in your area and you want to use the pit method, you can gather river rocks and preheat them.

Note: Whether using river rock or lava rock, choose rocks that are uniform in size.

River rocks often crack and even explode when first exposed to extreme heat. When this happens to rocks in an imu, stone splinters can be driven into the meat. If you preheat the rocks, however, you minimize the possibility of this occurring.

Prepare river rocks in this manner: select about 100 rocks weighing around 5 pounds each. At least 2 weeks before the luau, set the rocks in the hot sun and leave them there for a week. One week prior to the luau, preheat the rocks by placing them in a very hot open fire for 3 to 4 hours. Let the rocks cool completely and then store them in a dry place until you're ready to use them. Do not let them get wet.

A day or so before the luau, select a spot well away from any structures, foliage or other combustible materials and dig a hole 3 feet deep, 4 feet across and the length you will need for the size of your pig. Line the pit with fire brick (purchased at a specialty barbecue or fireplace store) or preheated rocks. This prevents the heat from being lost into the earth. Note: You'll need considerably more than 100 rocks if you're going to use them to line the pit.

Locate a wood pole or metal pipe which is about 3 inches in diameter and 5 or 6 feet long. Wrap a wad of burlap around one end of the pole, secure it with wire and place the pole into the center of the pit so that the burlap-wrapped end rests on the bottom of the brick-lined pit. This will be your means of lighting the fire.

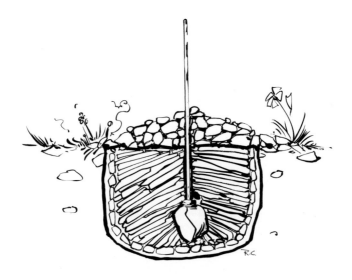

Around the pole at the bottom of the pit, stack a lot of kindling and wood in a pyramid shape. Make sure air can easily circulate around and between the pieces of wood. Stack the lava or preheated rocks on top of the wood.

Approximately 2 to 4 hours before the pig goes into the pit, pull the pole out of the pit, dip the burlap-wrapped end into kerosene or charcoal lighter fluid. **Do not use gasoline**. Carefully light the soaked burlap and insert the pole back into the hole. This will start the fire.

Let the fire burn down. The fire is ready when the coals are glowing and the rocks are red hot.

The Gravel Alternative

Robert E. Rust (Professor Emeritus, Meat Science) suggests using gravel instead of rocks in the pit. He recommends preparing a pit measuring 3 feet deep, 30 inches wide and the length to accommodate the pig. Build a fire in the pit using enough dry hardwood to equal about $2^1/_2$ times the volume of the pit. Allow the wood to burn 4 to 6 hours. When the pit is half full of hot coals, level the coals and remove any unburned chunks of wood. Cover the hot coals completely with a 2-inch layer of pea gravel.

How to Prepare and Roast the Pig

Rub liberal amounts of rock salt into the cavity of the pig carcass. The National Pork Producers Council in Des Moines, Iowa, suggests using caution when adding spices, seasonings and sauces to pit-roasted pork because the flavor will be retained and even intensified within the pit. Most people agree that the flavor of the pork by itself is an unforgettable taste treat without adding other flavorings.

Protecting your hands by wearing heavy oven mitts, fill the carcass with some of the hot rocks from the pit (no need to do this if you're using the gravel method). Tie both hind legs securely to both front legs. Line a large section of chicken wire with banana leaves, corn husks or aluminum foil and enclose the entire pig in the lined chicken wire. Note: Before closing the wire around the pig, you can add yams, fish or ears of corn wrapped in foil or corn husks.

When using the hot rock method, remove any wood fragments and spread the hot rocks out in the bottom of the pit creating a bed to accommodate the carcass. Cover the ashes and hot rocks with green corn leaves

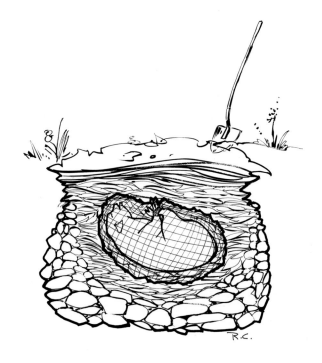

and husks, ti leaves or banana stumps and leaves. Some folks also use grass cuttings. Lay the pig (which is enclosed in chicken wire) on the leaves and husks. Cover the pig with more thick layers of husks and leaves.

Lay moistened lengths of burlap or gunny sacks over the second layer of leaves and cover the entire pit with a large piece of wet canvas. Carefully shovel dirt onto the canvas until the pit is completely covered. You do not want any steam escaping from the pit during the roasting process. If you notice steam escaping, quickly cover the area with dirt being careful not to let dirt trickle into the pit. Generally, it will take about 5 hours to cook a 100-pound pig by this method.

For the gravel method, Rust suggests omitting the leaves, wet gunny sacks and canvas. Simply place the carcass on a sheet of 2 x 4 inch welded wire, lower it into the pit and cover the pit with galvanized roofing which is supported on pipe or steel posts to keep it above the pig. Cover the roofing with a foot or more of dirt. According to Rust, a pig with the skin on needs no additional covering. Allow the pig to cook for 12 hours. Rust says this cooking time would be appropriate for any size pig the pit will accommodate, "because," he explains, "the larger the pit, the greater the volume of hot coals."

Check List for Cooking in a Pit

Fire bricks or river rocks to line the pit (preheat rocks).

- Lava rocks, gravel or river rocks for heat (preheat river rocks).

- Pole, 5 or 6 feet long and 3 inches in diameter.

- Wad of burlap.

- Wire for fastening the burlap to the pole and securing the chicken wire around the carcass.

- Kerosene or charcoal lighter.

- Kindling and fire wood (or dry hardwood).

- Matches.

- Chicken wire large enough to envelop whole carcass.

- Heavy oven mitts.

- Shovel.

- Burlap or gunny sacks (enough to cover the carcass).

- Green corn leaves and husks, ti leaves or banana stumps and leaves.

- Canvas the size of the pit opening. Or enough galvanized roofing material to cover the pit opening.

Pig on a Spit

If you're not daring enough or do not have enough space, assistance or support to attempt roasting a pig under the ground, you may want to try cooking it on a spit.

It may be necessary to remove the head to successfully cook a pig on a spit. Run the spit lengthwise through the balance point of the pig carcass and secure the carcass on the spit with wire or wire mesh. Be prepared to adjust the wire to fit the carcass as it shrinks in the cooking process.

To prevent flare-ups, the Iowa Pork Producers Association in Clive, Iowa suggests arranging charcoal briquettes in 2 rows about 12-15 inches apart under the spit and the length of the pig and placing a drip pan under the pig between the rows of charcoal to catch the drippings.

Once the pig is placed over the coals, cover the pit or barbecue with a metal hood, enclosing the pig entirely. If you don't have access to a hood, construct one by cutting a clean 55-gallon drum in half lengthwise. (Remove one end of each barrel half and weld these halves together to make a larger hood.) Or, for a smaller barbecue, build an A-shaped hood of wood and line it with foil.

Drill a small hole in the hood and insert the end of a large meat thermometer. The gauge remains outside the hood for convenient viewing. Check the thermometer frequently. While some folks keep the inside temperature of their barbecue at 200 - 250°F, others have good results at 180° (pig takes longer to cook) or even

325°(pig cooks faster).

If the spit is not motorized, turn the pig by hand every 20 minutes. Watch coals constantly. Don't allow flames to flare up. Smoldering coals are all that is necessary to roast a 35-pound pig on a spit in a covered barbecue in 4 hours.

If money is scarce and creativity high, you might build your own free-standing spit. Assemble two sturdy tripods using poles or lengths of pipe. Incorporate a method of adjusting the distance between the pig and the coals and a means of easily turning the spit. To shorten the cooking time, build oven walls around the pig using concrete blocks or metal sheets.

When is the Pork Done?

The National Pork Producers Council now suggests that for medium doneness the internal temperature of pork need only reach 160°F or 170°F for well done pork. According to Robin Kline, M.S., R.D., director of the Pork Information Bureau for the NPPC, these changes reflect new research based on the fact that pork products are leaner and more healthful today.

Robert Rust concurs and further explains, "While 160°F is a safe temperature for roast pork, a temperature of 170°F for a whole pig will produce a product of superior acceptance."

Above the Ground Pit Barbecue

Most people seem to enjoy the flavor pork fat gives the meat. Those who prefer a drier, less fatty meat, however, may wish to prepare their pig in an above-ground pit.

Build a Pit Above the Ground

Partially bury fourteen (14) 8 x 8 x 16-inch cement blocks in a rectangle shape placing 3 blocks across each end and 4 blocks along the sides. (Adjust the pit according to the size of your pig.) Stack additional blocks 3 rows high on the sides of the pit and 2 rows high on the ends.

Next, construct a 2-piece wire mesh rack to envelope a pig that is split down the middle and laid out flat. (Head and legs removed). This pig rack is a larger version of those used for grilling hamburgers.

Suggestion: Use 3/4-inch metal rod in constructing the frame for the rack. Extend 2 rods approximately 12 feet at each of the 4 corners. These extensions will allow the rack to rest on the blocks over the coals and will also be used as turning grips. By placing the turning grips on the end blocks, the pork is closer to the coals. When the heat is more intense, raise the rack by resting the grips on the higher side.

Start the fire in a small ring of rocks outside the pit. When the fire turns to coals, place 1/2 shovel full of coals inside the cooking pit at each corner.

Remove the head and legs of the pig and split the entire carcass down the middle so it lies out flat (butterfly fashion). Secure the pig within the rack and lay it across the pit allowing the extensions to rest on the low end of the bricks. Turn the pig every 20 minutes and, using a new household mop, baste the meat with salt water each time you turn it. (Salt water will draw the fat from the pork.) Add 1/2 shovel full of coals to each of the 4 corner spots as needed. With the open pit method, a 200-pound pig will take up to 18 hours to cook.

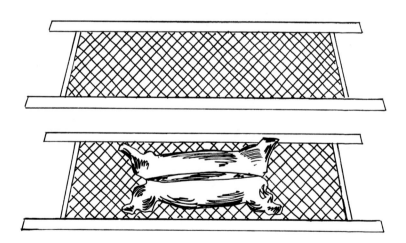

Basted Pork Barbecue

For more succulent, well-flavored pork, place 8 x 8 x 16 inch cement blocks 2 blocks high and the size you will need for your pig. Fill any gaps between the blocks with dirt. Build a fire within the pit and let it burn until only coals remain. Place a grate over the fire letting it rest on the bricks. Rub the cavity of a whole pig with salt and Five Spice (available in the Oriental section of most markets). Place a stick crossways inside the cavity to hold it open. Lay the pig on the grate and baste with this sauce using a child's toy mop.

> 5 cups water
> $3/4$ cup vinegar
> $1/3$ cup Five Spice
> salt (optional)
> pineapple juice (optional)

Cover the roasting pig with a large metal hood. Turn and baste the pig every 20 minutes. With this technique, you can cook a 200-pound pig in approximately 16 hours. (Some people turn the pig just once – at the halfway point in the cooking process.)

To make a delicious gravy from the remaining basting mixture, add 2 tablespoons sugar and 1 cup pineapple juice. Place the mixture in a saucepan on the stove and cook it down for approximately 1 hour. Add cornstarch to thicken slightly.

The turning and basting of the pig can be one of the highlights of the luau. Everyone wants to watch the roasting process and some are eager to participate. Getting help for this task is usually no problem.

The Redwood Box Cooker Method

Paul Brown of Montana cooks whole pigs and quarters of beef in specially designed redwood boxes. He says that his pigs come out moist and juicy with a crispy outer skin which his German friends, in particular, love to eat.

Using 2" (thick) x 12" (wide) redwood boards, Brown constructed a box measuring 51 1/2 inches long, 29 inches wide and 24 inches deep. He added 1/8 inch steel angles on the outer edges of the corners of the box for reinforcement and 1/4 inch steel rod handles for ease in moving the box. To keep the box off the ground, he nailed 4" by 4" pieces of redwood on the bottom.

Into the bottom of the box goes a 46 1/4 inch by 22 1/2 inch by 3 inch deep metal drip pan with 1/4 inch steel rod handles.

The roasting pan goes next and can be constructed of a heavy metal screen, mesh or grate welded to an 1/8 inch steel frame. (Brown used variegated steel.) This tray measures 41 inches by 20 inches with 3-inch legs to keep the meat out of the drippings. And it has 1/4 inch steel rod handles for ease in removing the roasted pig from the cooker.

With this roasting method, the heat is generated from above the meat. The charcoal pan (constructed of 1/8 inch steel) has an inside measurement of 42 inches by 20 inches by 3 1/4 inches deep and it has a 2 3/4 inch lip all the way around to hold it to the top of the box. This tray also has 1/4 inch steel rod handles.

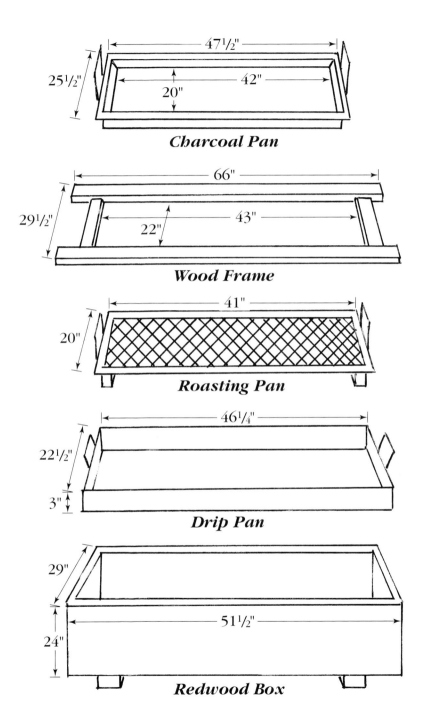

For the top of the box, Brown constructed a wood frame measuring 66 inches by 29 1/2 inches from 2 x 4 inch redwood. The opening measurement of this piece is 43 inches by 22 inches and it is placed on the top edge of the box to help seal in the heat. The charcoal pan sits within the opening of this top piece.

If you're not able to construct the metal pans yourself, Brown suggests having a local machine shop form and weld them for you. This is what he did and he paid around $125 each.

Brown cooks a 75 to 85 pound pig for about 7 hours at a temperature of 300 - 350°F by this method.

He monitors the temperature inside the cooker using a needle thermometer which is similar in design to a meat thermometer. He places the pointed end of the thermometer through a 1/4" hole about half way down the side of the roasting box with the dial sticking out so he can keep an eye on the temperature. If the temperature registers much over 350°, Brown lifts the charcoal tray off of the cooker for a few minutes.

Oven Roasted Suckling Pig

If the weather doesn't permit an outdoor event and you are entertaining a small group, roast a piglet in your oven.

For 10 guests, select a pig weighing about 20 pounds. Wash the pig in cold water and dry. Sprinkle the inside of the carcass with salt or rub the inside with a cut clove of garlic. You may stuff the piglet using 3 boxes of prepared stuffing. Add fruit or make a sausage stuffing. (Follow the directions for stuffing a pig on next page.)

Place a corn cob or block of wood in the pig's mouth to hold it open for an apple. Brush the skin with butter or oil and cover the pig with cheesecloth dipped in salad oil to prevent the skin from burning or cover it with a paper grocery bag when it starts to brown. Cover the ears with foil. Lift the cheesecloth wrapping several times during roasting to prevent it from sticking to the skin.

Place the piglet belly down on a wire rack in a roasting pan and roast at 350°F for around 3 1/2 hours or until the internal temperature reaches 165 – 170°F.

To serve, lay the pig on a platter of lettuce leaves, place a red apple in its mouth and dress it with a necklace "lei" of fresh cranberries.

Stuffing a Pig

You may want to stuff the pig before cooking it. Use 4 boxes of prepared dressing for a 50-pound pig. Mix stuffing so that it is on the dry side. Add pineapple, raisins, onions, celery and/or apples. If you want your onions and celery soft, sauté them before adding them to the stuffing.

To stuff a pig, line the cavity with a piece of cheesecloth. Place stuffing loosely into the cheesecloth and tie the ends of the cloth to hold the stuffing in place. Poke small holes along both sides of the outer edge of the abdominal skin, run pieces of light-weight wire through these holes and draw them together to close the cavity.

Serving the Pork

In the majority of our luau experiences, the pork was far too tender to consider carving. It fell off the bones in moist chunks and that is the way we served it. According to the North Carolina Pork Producers Association, in the south, they "pick" the pork from a slow-roasted pig and eat it "with great gusto."

Marvin Walter, however, feels that "laying the roasted pig out for show and carving is a critical part of the party." He suggests, before removing the pig from the pit or barbecue, that you cover a cutting board or table with foil and then create a decorative ring of pineapple, orange, lemon and apple slices around the outside.

Take great care in removing the pig from the pit or other cooking apparatus as the meat will most likely fall off the bone. Place the pig feet down within the ring of fruit. Let the pork sit for 20 minutes.

Walter then recommends cutting through the skin at the pig's tail end and vertically along the top center line to the head. Then cut horizontally down at the far posterior end of the carcass at the back edge of the ham and at the front edge of the blade bone at the shoulder on one side of the pig. Peel the skin back from that side only and proceed to carve and serve the meat. According to Walter, this process maintains the appearance of the pig longer and keeps the meat warm and moist until it is served.

I recommend that you serve the first helping of meat to your guests rather than allowing them to serve themselves. The pork will be the most popular item on the menu and you want to make sure there is enough to go around.

At our first luau, we mistakenly served the food buffet-style. Those who were first in line piled their plates high with meat and the folks at the end of the buffet line missed out. After that, we always served a reasonable, but generous, first portion and left seconds up for grabs.

In the event that you have meat left over, wrap and freeze it as soon as it cools. One day soon you can thaw it and make a pot of chili verde for an intimate party gathering.

Tips for Tending the Pig

As you can see, although it's not complicated, cooking a luau pig is a time-consuming task. And you're probably wondering who's going to be up all day and night preparing the pit and monitoring the roasting pig. Make this a group effort.

Invite your co-hosts/hostesses over the night before the luau. While some of you are mixing the punch ingredients, decorating, making leis and adding the finishing touches to the side dishes, others can prepare the fire pit and start the pig cooking.

Someone will have to watch the pit for flare-ups while it's burning down and, in some cases, turn and baste the pig every 20 minutes. Depending on the size of the pig and the time you plan to eat, some of this preparation may begin the night before and continue throughout the wee hours of the morning. Consequently, someone will have to be awake and alert during the process.

Make it a camp out. While 2 people sleep, 2 can take their turn watching the fire pit or rotating the pork. You can repay the efforts of these true friends the next morning by offering a filling but easy-to-prepare breakfast which includes plenty of hot coffee.

6. Entertaining Your Luau Guests

What is a visit to the Islands without being treated to a performance by grass-skirted hula dancers swaying to the sweet sounds of Hawaiian music . . . or natives telling Island stories through rhythmic dances while colorfully clad musicians skillfully play ukuleles and shake *uli ulis* (feather gourds)?

Invite Hawaiian dancers to perform at your luau. If you aren't acquainted with someone who knows Island dances, start networking. Ask friends if they can recommend a Hawaiian dancer. Contact dance studios. One of the instructors might perform for a small fee or there might be a couple of students who would love to dance for the experience and exposure.

Contact the local art center, theater group and civic or senior organizations. You might discover some potential entertainment. Up until the time of her death at the age of 88, Ethel Eddy headed up a group of senior citizens who performed Hawaiian dances for fun and a donation to the local senior citizen center.

You and your co-hosts/hostesses could learn a couple of easy Hawaiian dances yourselves and participate in the performance. If you can't find a teacher, invest in or rent a Hawaiian dance video and let it teach you the hula. Or borrow a book on Island dances from the library.

Group participation is always fun. As part of the program, plan to provide dance lessons B a simple hula for the women (*Little Brown Gal*, for example) and a rhythmic native dance for the men guests.

Consider alternative entertainment. If you know someone who sings, ask them to learn a couple of Hawaiian songs to share. If you've hired a band of musicians, have them rehearse at least a few Hawaiian tunes to play throughout the day. We once had a performance by a friend who was taking belly dancing lessons. It didn't quite fit the Hawaiian theme, but her performance was an unforgettable hit nonetheless.

Contact a local storyteller's group and invite some of them to share Hawaiian tales. Arranging for group participation would be a plus.

Ask a clever writer to create a comical script using a lot of words from the Hawaiian language. This could be performed by practiced individuals or through group participation.

For a more authentic atmosphere, provide Hawaiian background music throughout the luau. Buy records, tapes or CDs or borrow them from friends or the library. Start your search for Hawaiian music well in advance of the event in case it's difficult to locate or you have to order it.

7. A Hawaiian Language Lesson

The melodic Hawaiian language is one of the most beautiful yet it's fairly easy to learn. The Hawaiian alphabet consists of only 12 letters. The 7 consonants are: H, K, L, M, N, P and W. The vowels, A, E, I, O and U, are pronounced: ah, ay, ee, oh, oo. In the Hawaiian language, every word and every syllable ends with a vowel. Vowels often appear together in words and are pronounced separately.

Following is a list of some of the more familiar Hawaiian words, their pronunciation and their meaning:

Aikane (ay-kah-nay) - friend
Aloha (ah-lo-ha) - love, affection, welcome, good-bye
Anuenue (ah-noo-eh-noo-eh) - rainbow
Aole (ah-oh-lay) - no
Auwe (au-way) - ouch!
Haole (haw-lay) - foreigner, non-Hawaiian
Halakahiki (hah-la-ka-hee-kee) - pineapple
Hana (hah-nah) - work
Hauoli la hanau (hah-oo-oh-lee la ha-nah-oo) - happy

birthday
Hoolaulea (hoh-oh-la-oo-lay-ah) - festive gathering, party
Huhu (hoo-hoo) - angry
I'a (ee-ah) - fish
Imu (ee-moo) - underground oven
Ipo (ee-poh) - sweetheart
Kala (kah-lah) - money
Kamaaina (kah-mah-eye-nah) - old-timer
Kane (kah-nay) - male, husband
Kanaka (kah-nah-kah) - man
Kapu (kah-poo) - forbidden, keep out
Kaukau (Kah-oo-kah-oo) - food, meal
Keikamahine (kay-ee-kah-muh-hee-neh) - girl, daughter
Keiki (kay-ee-kee) - child
Keikikane (kay-ee-kee-kah-neh) - boy, son
Kope (koh-pay) - coffee
Laiki (lay-kee) - rice
Lio (lee-oh) - horse
Lolo (low-low) - stupid
Luau (loo-ah-oo) - feast, leaves of taro
Mahalo (mah-ha-loh) - thank you
Maia (may-ah) - banana
Malihini (mah-lee-hee-nee) - stranger, newcomer
Mele Kalikimaka (may-lay kah-lee-kee-mah-kah) - Merry Christmas
Mele (may-lay) - song
Mo'opuna (Moh-oh-poo-nuh) - grandchild
Nani (nah-nee) - beautiful
Nui (noo-ee) - great, big
Okole (oh-koh-ley) - bottom
Okole maluna (oh-koh-ley Mah-loo-nah) - bottoms up (a toast)
Onaona (oh-nah-oh-nah) - lovely
Ono ono (oh-noh oh-noh) - delicious
Pau (pah oo) - finished
Papale (Pah-pah-lay) - hat
Paniola (pah-nee-oh-lah) - Hawaiian cowboy

Pilikia (pee-lee-kee-ah) - trouble
Pololi (poh-loh-lee) - hungry
Pua (poo-ah) - flower
Punee (Poo-neh) couch
Pupu (poo-poo) - appetizer
Pupule (poo-poo-lay) - crazy
Wahine (wah-hee-nay) - female
Wela (way-lah) - hot
Wela Kahao (way-lah kah-ha-oh) - whoopee
Wikiwiki (wee-kee-wee-kee) - quick, hurry up

Here is a list of some of the more common American names translated into Hawaiian. Locate other names as well as more information about the Hawaiian language through your local public library or by writing to the Hawaiian Chamber of Commerce at Dillingham Building, 735 Bishop Street, Honolulu, Hawaii 96813.

Women		Men	
Alice	Aleka	Adam	Akamu
Amy	Eme	Allen	Alena
Barbara	Palapala	Arthur	Aka
Becky	Peke	Ben	Peni
Beverly	Peweli	Bill	Pila
Carol	Kalola	Bob	Lopaka
Charlotte	Halaki	Charles	Kale
Deborah	Kepola	Daniel	Kaniela
Diane	Kiana	David	Kawika
Donna	Kona	Dennis	Kenika
Dorothy	Kolokea	Dick	Likeke
Elizabeth	Elikapeka	Don	Kona
Emily	Emele	Earl	Ele
Erica	Elika	Edward	Ekewaka
Frances	Palani	Eric	Elika
Gail	Kaila	Eugene	Iukini
Gloria	Kololia	Frank	Palani
Helen	Helena	Gary	Kali

Irene	Ailina	George	Keoki
Janice	Kanike	Gerald	Kelala
Jacqueline	Keakalina	Glenn	Kelena
Jenny	Kini	Gordon	Kolekona
Joan	Ioana	Hank	Haneka
Judy	Lukiki	Henry	Hanale
Karen	Kalini	Howard	Haoa
Kathleen	Kakalina	James	Kimo
Laura	Lala	John	Keoni
Linda	Lika	Joseph	Iokepa
Louise	Luika	Keith	Kika
Marcia	Malakia	Kenneth	Keneke
Margaret	Makaleka	Lawrence	Lauleneke
Mary	Malia	Mark	Maleko
Michelle	Mikala	Martin	Makini
Nancy	Naneki	Michael	Mikala
Olivia	Oliwia	Ned	Neki
Pamela	Pamila	Nicholas	Nikolao
Patricia	Pakelekia	Norman	Nolemana
Penny	Piliki	Owen	Owene
Rachel	Lahela	Paul	Paulo
Rose	Loke	Peter	Pekelo
Sarah	Kala	Philip	Pilipo
Sharon	Kalana	Richard	Likeke
Stephanie	Kekepania	Roger	Lokela
Susie	Kuke	Ronald	Lonala
Theresa	Keleka	Samuel	Kamuela
Vickie	Wikolia	Thomas	Kamaki
Virginia	Wilikinia	Timothy	Kimokeo
Winifred	Winipeleke	Wayne	Wene
Yvonne	Iwone	William	Wiliama

Conceptually, you may be able to pretty closely translate the American names of your guests into Hawaiian yourself. What do you do with letters that are not part of the Hawaiian alphabet B, F, G, S, T, V, for example? Use this key to help in the translation:

English Letter	Hawaiian Letter
C, D, G, T, Th, S, X, Z	K
J	K or I
R	L
B, F, Fr	P
V	W
Y	E

For example, the Hawaiian name for Sandra might be, Kanekela. (Notice that the S and D have been replaced by K, instead of an R we used an L, and we added vowels between the consonants.) Brittany might translate into Pilikani; Brian -- Pilane; Lou Ann -- Lui Ane; Robin -- Lopine; Victor -- Wikoli, and so forth.

Give your luau an added air of authenticity by incorporating the Hawaiian language into your party agenda. Here are a few ideas:

- Prepare name tags with the guests' names written in Hawaiian

- Teach each guest a couple of Hawaiian words and encourage them to use these words throughout the day and to trade words with the other guests.

Create contests and games:

- The guest who has learned the most Hawaiian words by the end of the evening wins a prize. (He/she must also know the meaning of each word.)

- The best teacher wins a prize, too. This is judged by the number of people who learned the Hawaiian words that a particular guest was teaching.

- Reward the person who creates the best sentence

using only Hawaiian words.

- Write a sentence in Hawaiian on a large blackboard, and give a prize to the guest who comes closest to deciphering the phrase.

- Provide a list of guests' first names in Hawaiian and challenge your guests to find their own names on the list.

- Pin names (in Hawaiian) at random on each guest and ask everyone to search until they locate their own name. Those who find their own names within a certain length of time win a fresh flower to put behind their ears or earn a spot at the front of the food line. (This is a good mixer activity.)

Prizes can include: Hawaiian posters, flower arrangements used in decorating, fresh flower leis, decorated straw hats and Hawaiian music tapes.

8. Sundry Host & Hostess Tips

No matter how thoroughly you plan your luau, expect the unexpected because it will happen. A co-host will be called out of town on business and be unable to pick up the pig and make the fried rice. There will be a mix-up with the rental agency regarding the tables and chairs. The puppy will chew a hole in your new party sandals. Friends from out-of-town will call and ask to stay with you while you're trying to get things ready for the luau.

Be prepared and be flexible:

1. Do as much of the preparation as you can ahead of time because there WILL be unexpected details to take care of at the last minute.

2. Solicit help.

3. Take advantage of spare minutes to rest and regroup.

4. Remember, this is a party – have fun with it!

Following are some of the areas where you can use last minute assistance:

- Yard clean-up. Hire a couple of neighborhood kids to rake leaves, sweep the patio and clean the pool. Ideally, you'll have planted new flowers and completed any major yard maintenance weeks earlier.

- Cutting up the fruit and keeping food platters and the punch bowl full. Pay a couple of college students $6.00 an hour to handle these kitchen duties for a few hours during the day of the luau. If you hire them to come in an hour or so before the luau, this will free you up to take last minute calls from guests needing directions and to dress for the party.

- Parking. If you anticipate a parking problem, ask a couple of responsible young men or women to run a shuttle for guests or offer valet parking.

Note: It would be nice if the helpers wore Hawaiian attire.

How to Handle Difficult Guests

Some guests require more attention than others. While some mingle and make themselves comfortable, others will come to you with all kinds of questions; "Where shall I store my video camera when I'm not using it?" "Do you have a cloth and some distilled vinegar? George just spilled punch on his shirt." "Where can I find an ashtray?" "Can I borrow a towel? I'd like to go for a swim and I forgot mine." "John pushed me in the pool. Do you have something I can wear while my clothes dry?" And even this – "Peggy, I need to talk to you in private for a few minutes. Ronnie and I just had a fight and I need someone to talk to."

A good host/hostess will:

- Try to spend some time with each guest throughout the course of the party.

- Introduce guests to one another and encourage conversation between them by bringing to light something they might have in common or that would be of interest to both of them. For example: "Bob, this is Grace. She and her husband just bought the house across the street from your parents." or "Susan, do you remember the trip we took last April? This is the travel agent who arranged it for us." or "Kevin, Stanley is our new chamber chairman."

Tips for Staying Cool

The luau is two days away. It's been your whole focus for weeks. You've been involved in the planning and preparation of every detail. Now you just want to relax and enjoy the party, but you're starting to dread it. You wish it was over. You're edgy and tense. You may be suffering from luau-overload or pre-party burn-out.

- Shift your focus for a few hours or, if possible, a few days. Treat yourself to a massage, an hour at the beach or at the mall or whatever sort of distraction you enjoy and find most relaxing.

- Learn a relaxation technique and use it a couple of times a day throughout your busiest times. As an example, simply sit in a quiet room with your eyes closed and visualize a calming scene B ocean waves lapping at a white sand beach, a meadow of tall grass swaying in a gentle breeze or a dense fern forest.

• If you get little butterflies or feel giant waves of anxiety whenever you think about the party, try a visualization technique. Visualize your luau being perfect from start to finish. Imagine yourself being the ideal host/hostess. The food is absolutely delicious. Everyone is having a wonderful time. This is clearly the event of the season. Believing is seeing!

• Make the planning of the luau as much fun as the luau itself by keeping things light, being flexible and not taking anything too seriously.

• Take all precautions necessary for the guests' safety: fill in gopher holes, keep small children away from the pool and the pig cooker, make sure chairs and tables are sturdy and in good repair and take care in food handling and preparation.

Your demeanor will set the tone for the climate of your luau. So relax and allow it to be all that it can be. Aloha makamaka. Farewell, friend.

Index to Recipes

Popular Island Recipes
Easy Island Meatballs 27
Salmon Stuffed Tomatoes 28
Pineapple-Shrimp Pupus 28
Sweet and Sour Pork 29
Fried Rice 30
Long Rice 31
Chicken Hawaiian 32
Linaka's Honey Dressing 33
Easy Hawaiian Fruit Salad 34
Luau Fruit Salad for 50 34
Make it Easy On Yourself Fruit Salad for a Crowd 35
Crab-Rice Salad 35
Yams 36
Corn on the Cob 36
Ethel's Laulaus 37
Pork Barbecue Sauce 55

Delightful Hawaiian Punch Recipes
Fruity Island Punch 40
Kahlua Punch 40
Pineapple Daiquiri 41
Chi Chi 41